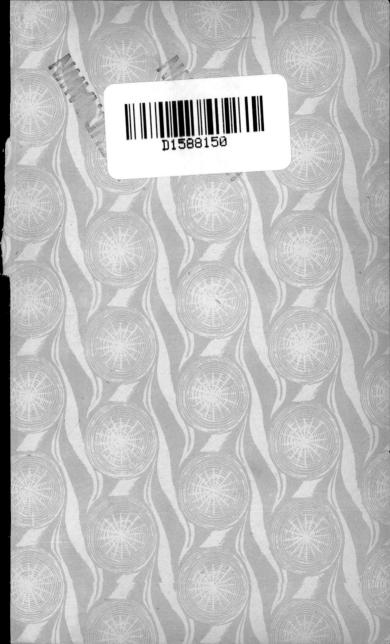

D1588150

Everyman, I will go with thee, and be thy guide.
In thy most need to go by thy side.

This is No. 792 of Everyman's Library.

EVERYMAN'S LIBRARY
EDITED BY ERNEST RHYS

POETRY & DRAMA

POEMS AND PROPHECIES
BY WILLIAM BLAKE · EDITED
BY MAX PLOWMAN

WILLIAM BLAKE, born in 1757. Apprenticed as an engraver to James Basire, 1771–8. Student at the Royal Academy, 1778. Kept a printseller's shop, 1784–7. Exhibited at the Royal Academy, 1780–1808. Died in 1827.

POEMS AND PROPHECIES

WILLIAM BLAKE

LONDON: J. M. DENT & SONS LTD.
NEW YORK; E. P. DUTTON & CO. INC.

INTRODUCTION

WILLIAM BLAKE has many titles to fame. He became a mark
for legend during his lifetime. People who knew him by repute,
or by some stray portion of his work, believed him to be an
eccentric; while those who knew him personally and were ad-
mitted to as much of his confidence as he could share, thought
him a man of genius. In passing, we may note that these two
opinions have persisted for a hundred years. Those who know
of Blake by repute still associate his name chiefly with eccen-
tricity; while those who are best acquainted with his work are
most convinced of his genius.

Apart from his achievements in art, Blake is entitled to
fame for his personal character. It is possible to hate his work,
but it is impossible to deny that he was a fine specimen of a
man, simple, honest and immensely courageous, of inflexible
purpose and tremendous energy, yet sensitive and gentle as
only the strong can be. His portrait stands out, clear and
boldly outlined, as one of the most admirable and (if we may
flatter ourselves for a moment) one of the most English among
men of letters. Touch him where you will, Blake rings true. Is
it Blake as a lover, becoming ill when his courtship is refused,
or as an artist, speaking his mind to the Rev. Dr. Trusler, or
as a friend, opening his heart to Captain Butts, or as a saint,
singing original hymns on his death-bed, every episode fits
the man, whose portrait Time has chiselled in marble and set
in the sunlight.

The details of his life are so well known, thanks to Alexander
Gilchrist and a host of dependent biographers, that it would be
tedious to give more than the barest outline here. He was born
at 28 Broad Street, Golden Square, London, on 28 November,
1757, and he died at 3 Fountain Court, Strand, on 12 August,
1827. Most of the years between these dates were spent in
London, the only memorable exceptions being the years 1800
to 1803, when he and his wife lived, under the patronage of
William Hayley, in a cottage at Felpham, near Bognor, on

the coast of Sussex. Blake's parents were what used to be called " lower middle class " folk. His father was a hosier, and the family consisted of several brothers and one sister. William never went to school, but at the early age of ten began to learn drawing at an academy in the Strand. He afterwards became an engraver by profession, and throughout his life engraving remained his principal means of livelihood. When he was nearly twenty-five he married Catherine Boucher, with whom he lived in close harmony for almost exactly forty-five years, when the poet died. Blake had no children.

Shortly after his marriage he seems to have been fairly prosperous, and in 1796 he received the important commission to design and engrave illustrations for the then popular Edward Young's *Night Thoughts*. This proved a disastrous enterprise. Blake made a prodigious number of drawings— so many we may be fairly sure half of them were the fruit of discontent with the other half—and those he finally engraved afford a striking example of the inability of Pegasus to draw a load of melancholy moral maxims. The failure of this publi-cation spoilt Blake's reputation as an artist for about ten years, during which period he made a great number of paintings and drawings for his ever-faithful patron Captain Butts, and did a lot of illustrative work for William Hayley of Felpham. His reputation, however, seems to have revived in 1808 on the strength of the highly successful illustrations to Blair's *Grave*; only to be ruined again by the exasperation he showed, at the time of his exhibition, on being excluded from the Academic Institutions of the day.

After that, Blake sought no more the favours of the public, but worked on, in poverty and solitude, executing com-missions of a very menial kind until the painter John Linnell discovered him and commissioned him to engrave the already completed series of drawings illustrating the *Book of Job*. When these were finished, and although they would not sell, Linnell again showed his admiration of his elderly friend's work by engaging him to make another series illustrative of Dante's *Divine Comedy*. It was upon this task that Blake was fully occupied when he died.

But it is not with Blake's title to fame as an artist that we are here chiefly concerned; moreover, that laurel has been generally accorded him. The prodigy who started his drawing lessons at the age of ten, began verse-making very soon afterwards, and is reputed to have been less than fourteen years old when he wrote the delicious song:

> *How sweet I roam'd from field to field*
> *And tasted all the summer's pride.*

These early poems were collected the year after his marriage and published, under the title *Poetical Sketches,* at the expense of a few kind and cultured friends to whom Blake had been introduced by the popular sculptor John Flaxman. Confessedly imitative work, derived in manner and in matter, these poems are now recognised as being one of the signal events in English literature. The amazing thing about them is the degree to which they break away from the poetic modes of the day, harking back with unstrained felicity to the finest lyrical poetry in the language. They are among the first blossoms of that fresh flowering of poetry, sometimes known as The Romantic Revival, which burst upon a prosaic world with the advent of Wordsworth, Coleridge, Shelley and Keats. Despite their derived nature, some of these poems are unsurpassed. The lines *To the Muses* and *To the Evening Star* are miraculous as all perfect poetry is miraculous. They have an effortless beauty such as is only achieved when the poet's conception is drenched in poetry and he speaks like a sibyl.

Why, it may be asked, was not Blake content to go on writing poetical sketches? If he here achieved perfect things, why should he have turned his back upon them, " twitch'd his mantle blue," and set out " To-morrow to fresh woods and pastures new "?

Well, the simplest answer to the question is the statement that there is a beauty of face and feature about an adolescent boy which, in the course of nature, quickly disappears, never to return; but if the boy should be fool enough to play Narcissus with his own fleeting beauty, nothing of his quality as a man can ever appear, but he will henceforth mime and mumble before us, a living effigy of his own past. Had Blake been content to copy the great dead when his days of apprenticeship were over, that false, fond note we all recognise so clearly on the lips of the artfully simple poet would have crept in: the youthful beauty would have become archaic, and Blake would have been the popular poet of his day: the highly respected, uncontroversial, standard poet of the literary cemetery.

When Blake was a child, he thought as a child; but when he

* 792

became a man, he put away childish things. It may seem a little paradoxical, but it is quite true to say that he put away childish things when he dropped his Shakespearean play, *King Edward the Third*; and became a man when he began

> *Piping down the valleys wild,*
> *Piping songs of pleasant glee.*

The years that divide the *Poetical Sketches* from the *Songs of Innocence* are the critical years of Blake's life, for in those years he found himself and discovered his theme. The *Poetical Sketches* are about anything and everything: here is a poet obviously looking for a theme: everything is his, but nothing belongs to him: he touches this and that string, runs an arpeggio here and strikes a chord there; but the harmonies are unrelated: no theme connects them. The lips are waiting for the live coal.

They were touched when Blake next wrote. From the *Songs of Innocence* to *The Ghost of Abel* he had one theme—the human soul. Cowper sang the sofa, Blake sang the soul. And the difference between Blake and his age—the difference between Blake and the fashionable poets of his youth is paralleled by the difference between a sofa and a soul.

Let no one despise the sofa or any of its counterparts in the modern kitchen or living-room. Poetry despises nothing, having a sense of values in which all is valuable. But the reason Blake has been so long misunderstood is that the same critical criteria will not serve for the analysis of the soul as will suffice to assess a sofa. When a poet is attempting to show objectively the movements of the soul, it is idle to expect from him the same kind of impression as eventuates from the portrayal of anything so objectively obvious as a sofa. Moreover, it is probable that when a poet first arises who has the great daring to launch out on to the deep waters of the human soul and let down his net for a draught, he may catch strange fish, unlike the carp, pike and sticklebacks of our sluggish rivers—fish we fail to recognise—fish we pronounce very ugly —fish we cannot cook, much less eat.

Far be it from the present writer to pretend that he is one to whom Blake's poetry is no mystery at all, but simple as pea-shelling, provided you take away the number you first thought of and multiply it by x. There have, unfortunately, been commentators upon Blake who have made similar claims, so that admirers of his more abstruse works must be prepared for the good-humoured shrug friends will accord them on the confession of their taste, or, as it will then be humorously described, want of taste. This is largely because the late Mr. E. J. Ellis (to whom we are all, nevertheless, greatly indebted, because of his faith and sincere admiration for Blake) printed a prodigious commentary which attempted to explain all the poems as if they were scientific works written in cypher that could only be completely understood by persons who practised divination.

Now a divining-rod of some sort is certainly essential to the enjoyment of Blake, for he is a symbolic poet even when he is writing about little lambs and little boys lost; but the divining-rod must be as simple and spontaneous in its action as the old dowser's hazel-stick, and Mr. Ellis associated it with the sort of horrific abstraction that does duty at séances for the evocation of spooks. Moreover, the essential matter to the commentary, Blake's text, was rather cavalierly treated; and when learned exposition was based upon actual misreading, the Philistines, who always believed Blake's attraction " sinister," began to rejoice, and have ever since shouted loudly at sight of anyone with the temerity to believe Blake always intended deeply, mattered greatly, and would eventually prove explicable down to the vagaries of his punctuation.

The great fish Blake drew out of the waters has been labelled with the generic name "prophetic works." It is a fairly harmless label, now applied to all those writings wherein Blake used strange names. We can but wonder what he would have thought of it. Perhaps he would have prophesied on it, declaring that it would pass out of use when we understood more precisely what we were talking about, and pointing out that he only described two of his books, *America* and *Europe*, as prophecies. But Leviathan was ever difficult to circumnavigate, and now it appears to lie on the beach of our understandings, brought inland a little nearer by every tide; becoming measurable as we lose our fear of its proportions; perceived not to be a fish at all, and ere long perhaps, to be cut up and used in every household as familiarly as the products of the great Moby Dick himself.

To mention this, as yet, is to anticipate editorial troubles. The point was that Blake was the poet of the soul. It is a distinction that needs explanation, since every poet is, in some measure, a poet of the soul. Even the singer of the sofa only uses that admirable and much to be lamented piece of furniture as a pretext. But where Blake differs from them all is in his objective treatment. He sings the adventures of the soul as Homer sang the adventures of Ulysses, or Chaucer the adventures of the Canterbury Pilgrims.

There were important reasons why the soul should have been his subject. The child of religious parents, he was born into an age when considerations for the external order of man had become so gross a bondage, the human soul was, as it were, consigned to the clerical department as that property of a man which chiefly required attention at the hour of death. Those who rejoiced in its evidences at other times were called Enthusiasts, and put into a category, much as we now put Bolsheviks. The god of the eighteenth century was Rational Behaviour. Man looked on man as homo sensual, and ordered his conduct accordingly. The poets wore a man-about-town air; and poetry, as we have since recognised it, was practically defunct. Pope summed the age up in a couplet:

> *Two principles in human nature reign:*
> *Self-love, to urge, and Reason, to restrain.*

Now, true as those principles are of all sentient beings, the possession of them does not greatly distinguish *homo sapiens* from the beast of the field, who, over-gorged with self-love, may be said to employ reason to restrain. A philosophy based upon so material a foundation gave little scope to a youth who had already celebrated a beauty not bounded by self-love on the one hand, or reason on the other. Blake had to choose between Spenser's Faerie Queene and Pope's Man—between winged Psyche and a respectable Silenus. The hour had struck; the soul awaited its champion, and Destiny could not have found a knight better fitted to rescue the Faerie Queene and slay the Blatant Beast than William Blake.

He began the quest with what have been called the " Tractates," *There is No Natural Religion* and *All Religions are One*. In these he is concerned to discover by logical deduction whether the soul exists, and if so, what is its nature. He discovers it to be an unreasoning super-sensuous entity, divine in its origin and destiny, whose perception and desire are infinite.

Having thus cleared the ground he begins with the *Songs of Innocence* to show what he describes as the original state of the soul, taking for his image of that perfect condition of being, the condition of childhood, a state of happiness, unity and self-enjoyment. Next he shows the soul about to leave its Eden, standing on the threshold of experience, full of intimations of that inevitable condition of mortality, but not yet entering (except imaginatively) upon a state from which its uninitiated consciousness withdraws in horror. This is *The Book of Thel*.

In the *Songs of Experience* the soul has eaten of the Tree of the Knowledge of Good and Evil, and left its Eden for ever. Its unity and integrity are destroyed. Experience is the contrary state to Innocence, a condition presaging disillusion, cruelty and death. Innocence was Heaven: Experience is Hell, and the two are left in contrast. But not for long. Blake's next great work was *The Marriage of Heaven and Hell*. Here the necessity for the contraries is discovered. They are welded for the purpose of creation and are perceived to be essential conditions of mortal life. Their marriage is the meeting of body and soul, celebrated many years later in another fashion, by the wonderful drawing for Blair's poem, *The Grave*.

And so the epic of the soul goes on. Blake regards life as the descent of spirit into matter in order that spirit may achieve form:

> *We like Infants descend*
> *In our Shadows on earth.*

Fully to understand these words is to obtain the key to Blake. He looked upon human life, not as the discontinuous appearance of phenomena, but as a particular manifestation of eternal being. Awake, we live in Eternity: asleep, we exist in Time. His idea of reality is the converse of the common idea. We speak of the reality of objects when we mean their material substance. That is precisely what Blake regards as their mortal disguise, or shadow. The living and informing spirit is for him the reality: the " corporeal " or " vegetative " form, the passing shadow.

Does the perception of the soul preclude sight of the body? That is the vexed question which is always asked in connection with Blake. That he saw the soul with extraordinary perception is not disputed: it emanates from his pictures

triumphing over a thousand obvious defects: it irradiates his
poetry giving life to his least utterance; but those who approach
the sanctuary of life by more pedestrian steps than Blake's
genius was ever capable of taking, are often antagonised by
certain of his sayings which seem to cast a slight upon the
sensuous impressions which are to them avenues of the soul.
"I assert for myself," he wrote towards the end of his life, when
his own " outward creation," or mortal body, was becoming
an encumbrance, " that I do not behold the outward creation,
and that to me it is hindrance and not action: it is as the dirt
upon my feet—no part of me." Does that mean that he had
no use for sun and moon, man and beast, and most of all
the human form? The question is an absurdity to which any
work of Blake's gives a proper answer. We have need to
understand with finer perception what he meant by " outward
creation." "A fool sees not the same tree that a wise man sees."
" The forms of all things are derived from their Genius." The
goal of all art is the same. To put division between soul and
body was never the purpose of him who gave them such a
royal marriage. But the outward form of the body falls into
the grave and rots. Blake's declaration is that this rotting
corpse is but appearance: had we eyes to see beyond its
" outward form " we should perceive the eternal renewal of
being, even in the grave.

The Marriage of Heaven and Hell was the result of a great
spiritual awakening in the mind of its author. With it Blake
freed himself from the cerements of organised religion. Now
he saw that the body, which religion had separated from the
soul and cast out, was in truth a vital portion of the soul—
that the senses, which religion viewed with suspicion and
mistrust, were "the chief inlets of soul in this age." In succeed-
ing books he began to inquire what was the enemy of true
religion, what was the buttress of false religion.

His answer is, the abstract idea of God: the substitution
of an invisible and unhuman deity (whose dwelling-place is
the void and whose chief attribute is his jealousy) for the
Divine Humanity, which is Blake's name for the spirit that
found its incarnation in the person of Jesus.

Blake believed that Man is the image of God. He believed
that the human was the divine—that man's divinity was
wholly according to the measure of his humanity. He believed
in the redemption of the world, by which he meant the

recognition by matter of its spiritual origin and destiny. That matter was farthest from the divine which was least conscious of its origin and destiny. Therefore, his world is graded according to consciousness; vegetable matter, being least conscious, is farthest from spiritual life: they are most alive in whom consciousness is most active. God and Man are identified:

> The worship of God is Honouring his gifts in other men, each according to his genius, and loving the greatest men best. Those who envy and calumniate great men, hate God, for there is no other God.

Again,

> God only acts & is in existing beings or men: an aphorism which finds a close parallel in Goethe's words to Eckermann nearly forty years later: " The divinity works in the living, not in the dead; in the becoming and changing, not in the become and the fixed."

The agency by which man achieves redemption is the Divine Imagination. This is again identified with the person of Jesus, who was for Blake, " God becoming as we are, that we may be as he is."

In his belief in the redemption of the world, it is interesting to compare Blake's attitude with Shelley's. Shelley gave to the cloud, the leaf, the wind, the sensitive plant and all " external nature," human attributes whereby their unconscious beauty becomes a conscious expression of love and harmony with man. In Shelley this passion for consciousness is unconscious; his love is blind while his faith is triumphant. But Blake had a clear perception of the way in which this redemption of "external nature " was to take place. He believed that as man was redeemed by God, or (to put it in another way) by the endowment of what may be literally described as super-natural consciousness, so nature would in turn be redeemed by the imaginative energy of the soul of man, man's love bringing to birth a new consciousness in nature. In the last words of *Jerusalem*, the sign of accomplished redemption is the humanising of all things—trees, metals, earth, the very stones—all are identified in human forms and endowed with the consciousness of man. In Shelley this personalising tendency was an instinctive desire: in Blake it was also an intellectual conviction. And whatever we may think of it, whether it appears as a pathetic and fantastic example of anthropomorphism, or a divine intuition of the truly prophetic soul, this idea must find its place in the mind of anyone wishing to understand Blake, for the simple and sincere expression of it recurs all through his work. Thus, with a literalness that appears at first sight to be almost childish, we find him in his illustrations to Milton's *L'Allegro* and *Il Penseroso* depicting mountains, rivers, trees, clouds and even the sun itself as human beings exercising their beneficial effects with the conscious intention of benign man.

The discovery of spiritual identities was Blake's idea of the poet's work. There is a passage in *The Marriage of Heaven and Hell* which has never received the attention it deserves for the light it casts upon Blake's apparently singular view of the poet's function. We say apparently singular because we believe it to be, in measure, an account of the practice of every poet, though less apparent in its workings as poetry is made to subserve the humbler of its privileges. Be that as it may, the passage gives a good account of Blake's own practice, and should be pondered before we fall foul of his persistent anthropomorphism.

The ancient Poets animated all sensible objects with Gods or Geniuses, calling them by the names, and adorning them with the properties, of woods, rivers, mountains, lakes, cities, nations, and whatever their enlarged & numerous senses could percieve. And particularly they studied the genius of each city & country, placing it under its mental deity. Till a system was formed, which some took advantage of & enslaved the vulgar by attempting to realise or abstract the mental deities from their objects: thus began Priesthood: Choosing forms of worship from poetic tales. And at length they pronounc'd that the Gods had order'd such things.

Thus men forgot that All deities reside in the human breast.

The animating of all sensible objects with Gods or Geniuses is a very exact description of what Blake attempted to do in all his longer work, and beginning with the human soul he discovered a variety of " Gods or Geniuses " (or what we should commonly call principles) active there. These gods, in their struggles for supremacy, carried on the wars of the spiritual world. To have described them by the names of their attributes would for him have been an inversion of his whole poetic intent. And since he needed names for their identification and none were ready to hand, Blake took the daring and, as some will think, disastrous step of giving them names according to his will. Or so it seems at present. Anyway, in these names lies the chief obstacle to the understanding of all his later work. It presents a difficulty not to be minimised. There exists at the present time no critical exegesis which even pretends to account for the peculiar names Blake gave to his "Gods or Geniuses," and whether a satisfactory explanation of their peculiarity will ever be found, no one can say. Meanwhile, the search for identification goes on, and a part (perhaps an illegitimate part) of the pleasure of reading Blake lies in the fact that his poetry is, as it were, virgin soil to every reader.

Not that his meaning is ever in doubt once the true and full significance of his words is appreciated. The difficulty is to obtain this full significance. Strange names apart, he uses many common words, and a still larger number of peculiar phrases, to connote uncommon meanings. For such words as eternity, reason, mystery, deceit, vision, imagination, he had extended and peculiar meanings which can only be appreciated by familiarity with the consistent workings of his mind; while phrases like "the Western path," "the gate of the Tongue," "soft Beulah's night," and "the dark Satanic mills," have precise and specific meanings, however amplified their purport may become by repetition.

The truth is that Blake had a powerful and independent mind, capable of moving with tremendous energy and fearless avidity; but owing to the poverty of his education in early days, he remained handicapped, having at his command but a poor equipment for the immense task he set himself. Thus, often enough, instead of being able to draw upon the riches of the language according to his need, after the manner of his revered Milton, he was driven to the expedient of doubling the meaning of a word of common currency, and even of divorcing it from its original meaning.

But this defect is more than compensated by the integrity of his thought and his infinite capacity for hard thinking. His mind moved at ease in atmospheres where even good intelligences begin to haver, and then gracefully to recline upon accepted opinions. Possibly because all his education was of his own providing, Blake never deluded himself into thinking other people's thoughts and fancying them his own. Perhaps because he knew himself to be wholly dependent upon his own mental efforts, he persisted in the attack upon mystery long after most of us have discovered our solitude and sought solace in tradition. He drove a lonely and a strange furrow; but he ploughed the earth deep and his line is perfectly straight. His analysis of Christianity should be sufficient evidence on this point.

Still, he is often baffling, and the human mind is so constituted that, directly it is baffled in its attempt at understanding, it is assailed by the temptation to fall into abuse. Living and dead, Blake has been roundly abused by people who have not had the intelligence even to appreciate what he was attempting. Those who want their reading to be repetitive of their own thoughts should avoid Blake: the daily newspaper is more profitable. On the other hand, those who believe beautiful things are hard may be encouraged to persist with Blake, if need be wrestling with him till the day breaks, in the assurance that he was no pettifogging mystifier, playing ducks and drakes with vague symbols, but a poet attempting the superhuman task of restoring to all things the mental deities which he believed systematised abstractions had banished.

Just as an example of the way his genius worked, let us glance at the book which follows *The Marriage of Heaven and Hell*.

Visions of the Daughters of Albion is an illustration of what happens to the soul when body and soul are divorced. There we are introduced to three characters: Oothoon, Theotormon and Bromion. The woman, Oothoon, is loved by Theotormon, but suffers outrage at the hands of Bromion, and nine-tenths of the poem is given up to her consequent lamentation. The poem has often been regarded as if it were merely a vulgar episode rather badly narrated. That it is something very different will be evident directly we discover who the three persons symbolise. This we may do by turning to the passage in *The Marriage of Heaven and Hell* which begins:

Those who restrain desire, do so because theirs is weak enough to be restrained; and the restrainer, or reason, usurps its place & governs the unwilling. And being restrained, it by degrees becomes passive, till it is only the shadow of desire.

There we have a concise description of the characters we are considering. Oothoon is desire, Bromion is reason, the restrainer: Theotormon is desire restrained till it is only the shadow of desire. They are three "Gods or Geniuses" warring in a human soul.

"Fear not them which kill the body." Blake was not primarily concerned with the physical implications of his poem, but that the human soul should be made to fall short of its destiny by the interposition of a negative reasoning faculty holding tyrannous sway over the delicate intuitive perceptions, this was for him blasphemy and outrage he protests against in words that send a shudder through the mind.

Blake described his work as "visionary and imaginative: it is an endeavour to restore what the Ancients called the Golden Age." Bearing in mind the passage we have quoted from *The Marriage of Heaven and Hell*, we may, perhaps, see more precisely what he meant. He conceived of the Golden Age as a time when men were conscious of the presence of the gods, not as monstrous creatures for ever at strife among themselves in cheerful disregard of puny mortals, but as the spiritual powers of man acting in known and appreciated harmony. He believed there was a time when these powers were evident to the enlarged and numerous senses of man, so that men were not beguiled by appearances, as they must always be beguiled when their powers of recognition lack the insight of vision. So he sought to bring again the recognition of spiritual powers by showing their activities, not superficially as we recognise them in material events, but perceptively, as we recognise them when we see the deep-seated causes of events. He did this in the belief that knowledge of the true causes would focus men's minds upon objects worthy of their contemplation and save them from the ruinous distraction which acceptance of material evidences begot. In a word, he believed that "all things work together for good to them that love God"; but to those whose God was Satan, who mistook the dead "become" for the living "becoming," all things acted in disastrous antagonism, and would continue to do so until insight (or the true perception of cause) superseded sight (or the photographic reception of appearances upon the mind's retina). The Golden Age would be restored when the Divine Imagination—love with insight and understanding— became the focal point of all man's contemplation; for then the warring gods in man would bow in adoration before the only power able to use and control his energies to the full.

So it is the old story of the strife of the gods that he tells. He has, however, the distinction of recognising the gods as operative in the human soul, and making them the subjects, and not the rulers of man. In the last " Night " of the unfinished work, *The Four Zoas,* the crucial moment in the redemption of Albion comes when the " Gods or Geniuses " of Heart, Mind, Body and Spirit, all recognise their subservience to the " Human form Divine," and the futility of setting themselves up, each in turn, as the supremely authoritative powers:

Luvah & Vala, henceforth you are Servants; obey & live.
You shall forget your former state; return, O Love, in peace
Into your place, the place of seed, not in the brain or heart.
If Gods combine against Man, setting their dominion above
The Human form Divine, Thrown down from their high station
In the Eternal heavens of Human Imagination—buried beneath
In dark Oblivion, with incessant pangs, ages on ages—
In enmity & war first weaken'd, then in stern repentance
They must renew their brightness & their disorganiz'd functions
Again reorganize, till they resume the image of the human,
Co-operating in the bliss of Man, obeying his Will,
Servants to the infinite & Eternal of the Human form.

There is no royal road to the difficult achievement of any large understanding of Blake. Our understanding of him being yet so partial, no attempt is made here to estimate either his comparative importance or the ultimate value of his contribution to human wisdom. Meantime, useful commentaries upon his writings exist, as well as some which are of little assistance. Among the almost indispensable guides may be mentioned particularly, Gilchrist's *Life,* Swinburne's *Critical Essay,* Mr. Foster Damon's *William Blake: His Philosophy and Symbols,* and Mr. Joseph Wicksteed's *Blake's Vision of the Book of Job.* They are all sympathetic and appreciative studies, free from what Blake once described as " confident insolence sprouting from systematic reasoning."

But in the last resort, Blake needs no commentator. The way to appreciation of his epic poems is very like the journey made by Meredith's traveller in the *Hymn to Colour,* who walked with Life and Death when Love appeared:

In that grey veil green grassblades brushed we by;
We came where woods breathed sharp, and overhead

> *Rocks raised clear horns on a transforming sky:*
> *Around, save for those shapes, with him who led*
> *And linked them, desert varied by no sign*
>   *Of other life than mine.*

For awhile we stumble along in the twilight catching a glimpse here or a sign there; but slowly, almost imperceptibly, light increases. There is a beam where before was darkness; a colour where all was lost in shadow. Gradually we become aware of a grand orchestration, and when the great purpose of all Blake's work rises before us, it is as if we watched the pageant of a new dawn.

>   *he leads*
> *Through widening chambers of surprise to where*
> *Throbs rapture near an end that aye recedes,*
> *Because his touch is infinite and lends*
>   *A yonder to all ends.*

It is thus that we now watch the spectacle, strange in its long delay, of the slow but ever increasing appreciation of Blake's work. Again and again this work has been measured by the rod of contemporary criticism and been found wanting. Yet with a persistence comparable to Blake's own, his work lives on, increasing in significance, growing in importance under our eyes, unfolding its dark meaning like some gorgeous flower slowly rising and bursting in beauty above a mass of undergrowth. Blake claimed the full prophetic powers of poetry, and his claim has already been justified. It is hardly possible to turn a page of his poems without meeting words which astonish by their appositeness to the discoveries of our own day. He was a psychologist who believed in dreams; a criminologist who saw the futility of revenge; a pacifist who understood the causes of war; an artist who believed that art mattered; a mystic who hated mystery; an educationist who believed in children; a Christian who believed in Jesus. In such beliefs and disbeliefs, which he held in his day almost alone, but which are now beginning to be shared by us all, we have signs of his spiritual insight and good assurance that the words he committed to such careful type were words worthy to be called both " inspired " and " prophetic."

Concerning this edition of his *Poems and Prophecies* it may be said that as the title follows his description of his work, so his authority has been accepted as final in respect of the comparative importance of his writings. Blake took particular care to set the seal of his authority upon what he wrote, by printing and illustrating it with unique care in his own stereo-type. By so doing he gave an importance to work completed in this manner which is denied to all other. Thus the acid test of Blake's approval has been made the criterion of this text. All those words which withstood the *aqua fortis* he was wont to pour upon his plates, leaving the type in high relief while the ground was burnt away, are here preserved. The rest are either printed as appendices or are omitted. Most of those omitted may be found in Dr. Sampson's Oxford edition of the *Poetical Works,* to which this volume is in many respects complementary.

To anyone versed in Blake's text there can be no question about the necessity for such discrimination. In the first place Blake made it himself. In the second, justice to any author demands that work he prepared for the press should be given precedence over casual memoranda. The fact that

> *Thy Friendship oft has made my heart to ache:*
> *Do be my Enemy—for Friendship's sake*

is a delicious heartfelt prayer, while such a line as

Go thou to Skofield: ask him if he is Bath or if he is Canterbury

looks like a very bad joke, will not excuse us for giving pre-ference to the first in an edition pretending to definition. (As a matter of fact, strictly speaking, the boot is on the other foot. *Thy Friendship oft,* etc., is, morally, a *bad* joke, while *Go thou to Skofield,* etc., is really a heartfelt prayer to the man of war, beseeching him to let us know whether his war is spiritual, like Canterbury, or " the war of swords and spears," typified by Roman Bath.)

While it is true that Blake's MS. book contains poems not printed by him which are of intrinsic beauty and biographical interest, it is important to notice that a number of these are rejected versions of the *Songs of Experience.* This was first pointed out to me by Mr. Joseph Wicksteed and is noteworthy because, however beautiful the rejected lyrics, only confusion can result if they are given importance equal to, or even greater than, poems Blake approved, engraved, illustrated, printed and coloured with his own hand. When editorship has assigned to each its proper place, criticism is free to prefer; but not before. That Blake ever intended to publish any more of the poems from the MS. book, beside those he used in the *Songs of Experience* or transferred to *The Pickering MS.*, is improbable, because there is evidence that he made his careful selection many years before he died.

This volume is, therefore, divided into three sections. Part I contains Blake's authoritative text; Part II. the most important of the works that remain in MS., with the exception of *The Four Zoas*, which is omitted owing to lack of room; Part III., the *Poetical Sketches*. These have been given an inferior place because they are obviously prentice work which Blake apparently put behind him as quickly as possible, being indifferent to, if not actually destructive of, the copies given him for circulation by the friends who printed and published the book.

The order of Part I. is believed to be strictly chronological, except that *The Book of Thel* was written before *Songs of Experience*. The date of *The Marriage of Heaven and Hell* is uncertain, but there can be little doubt that it was written after the *Songs of Experience*, for *The Marriage* represents a synthesis certainly not achieved when Blake was writing most of the *Songs*. The shadows that deepened in the *Songs of Experience* are dispelled by *The Marriage*, which marks the dawn of the day that gave birth to all the so-called Lambeth prophecies.

The structure of *The Marriage* is interesting. It consists of a poem as prologue, a prose argument composed in six chapters, and a song as epilogue. Blake indicates the beginning and end of these chapters by the use of designs for chapter headings and designs as colophons. Each chapter consists of a series of dogmatic statements, followed by a fanciful dithyramb which illustrates the foregoing statements, much as a parson's sermon illustrates his text. In the present volume, the end of a chapter is indicated by a double line, which has to do duty for one of Blake's beautiful designs; but here, for the first time in a transcript, the form of the work is made evident.

A Song of Liberty, often printed as a separate poem, is, without doubt, an integral part of *The Marriage of Heaven and Hell*. Swinburne knew this, but Mr. Ellis separated the *Song* on the ground that its symbolism was of a later date, and his example, unfortunately, has been followed. Apart from the fact that it is impossible to date Blake's use of symbols, the Argument that opens *The Marriage* is, equally, with *A Song of Liberty,* a symbolic poem. More than this, the *Song* is included in every known copy of *The Marriage,* which is paginated by Blake so that the *Song* appears on pages 25, 26 and 27 of this book. The *Song* sums up in symbol, what the prose passages of *The Marriage* say in logical statement and is its (to Blake) natural conclusion.

The three books *The Song of Los, The Book of Ahania* and *The Book of Los* are all dated 1795, but were probably written in the order given, the evidences for this being chiefly the manner in which the books were produced and finished.

Milton and *Jerusalem* are both dated 1804, a date that has nothing to do with the time when they were finished, but possibly may refer to the year when they were begun, or, it may be, the year in which they were conceived; for it will be remembered that Blake himself said:

Every Time less than a pulsation of the artery
Is equal in its period & value to Six Thousand Years,
For in this Period the Poet's Work is Done, and all the Great
Events of Time start forth & are conceiv'd in such a Period:
Within a Moment, a Pulsation of the Artery.

Jerusalem is certainly the later of these two epics.

The Gates of Paradise, a little book of engravings, first issued in 1793, is here reproduced in facsimile from a second printing about the year 1820. There were two distinct issues of this booklet. The first consisted only of the pictures and the inscriptions beneath them. This was inscribed on the title-page " For Children." The second issue is inscribed " For the Sexes," and to it Blake appended the couplets. There are differing impressions showing that Blake worked over the plates. The examples here reproduced are from a late copy, and differ in minor details both from the reproductions in the Nonesuch Edition and those published by Mr. Hollyer. Facsimile reproduction is essential in this instance, because without the designs the inscriptions are practically meaningless. And here we must say a word about the peculiar character of Blake's work in this respect.

Blake was both artist and poet, and the original manner in which he welded the two arts creates an insuperable difficulty in the way of a transcript version. Other poets, notably

D. G. Rossetti, have been artists also, but Blake is unique in making the two arts interdependent. From his first engraved plate of *There is No Natural Religion*, made probably in 1788, to the last, in which the ghost of Abel is seen breathing out revenge, in 1822, Blake's Poetical Works consist of a succession of words and designs which are not really separable. Again and again there is alternation between words that expand the meaning of a design, and designs that give to the words their complete significance. This is as true of *Songs of Innocence* as of *Jerusalem*. Hence it will be seen that no transcript of Blake's writings can lay claim to the word complete; nothing but a facsimile reproduction of the actual plates in colour is properly entitled to such a description, and at least one editor of Blake is hopeful that the day is not far distant when all transcripts will be regarded as merely supplementary to facsimile editions.

As regards the works omitted from this edition the most important of these is *Vala, or The Four Zoas, a Dream of Nine Nights*, begun at Lambeth about 1797, and probably concluded (although never revised and completed) at Felpham in 1803. *The Four Zoas* was probably begun with the title, *The Bible of Hell, in Nocturnal Visions Collected*, and may be accepted as fulfilment of Blake's promise to give the world The Bible of Hell. It is a work of great interest containing passages of Blake's finest poetry, and is equal in length to *Jerusalem*. Exigencies of space alone are responsible for its omission.

Other omitted poems are *Tiriel*, an early work existing only in MS., and *The French Revolution*, an historical poem, written in the manner of Ossian, and printed in proof only, in 1791; it was rediscovered by Dr. Sampson. Neither of these poems is of much more than biographical interest. Both are available in the Oxford *Blake*, which also contains the fine criticism of Chaucer from the *Descriptive Catalogue*. Blake's wonderful descriptive analysis of his now unhappily lost picture, " The Last Judgment," is here re-collected from photographs of the rough draft in the MS. Book (better known as *The Rossetti MS.*), but the so-called *Public Address* has not been included. The early satirical fragment in manuscript, *An Island in the Moon*, is also omitted as being of little importance. It is a hastily-written and incomplete piece of amusing nonsense.

Finally, coming down to dots and commas, the plate numbers have been added to the pages of *Milton* and *Jerusalem* because (owing to Blake's peculiar method of presenting his work by means of engraved plates) the logical sequence of the lines is sometimes broken by the insertion of additional plates. This is disconcerting, but perplexity is partially dispelled when we find that Blake was ready to sacrifice logical sequence if by so doing he might expand his theme. The practice, however, makes the addition of plate numbers essential to a transcript. For purposes of reference, line numbers are also added where necessary though the original books have none. Blake's capitals and peculiarities of spelling have been retained. The spelling matters little, and though the use of capitals (usually employed for emphasis) is sometimes idiosyncratic, it is often important. The reader will quickly learn to distinguish an appreciable difference of meaning between " the true Man " and " the True man," and fidelity in this respect is not pedantry.

On the other hand, Blake's punctuation cannot accurately be reproduced and his editors are here compelled to follow their own devices and promptly apologise for them. Facetious critics have inquired whether Blake's punctuation is not inspired. They are hereby advised in all seriousness to go to Blake's original pages to find out; for the efforts to punctuate Blake go to show that those who cannot read his lines as he wrote them will not be enabled to do so with the aid of the most skilful compositor. Indeed, while it is galling to one's ignorance to receive no assistance from Blake in this respect, it is not impossible that he deliberately punctuated, as in fact he wrote, so that those who only looked for logic should read to their own confusion. A chastening rule to be borne in mind throughout the study of Blake is that until his end is appreciated his means are unjustifiable.

The present form of this book would have been impossible but for valuable assistance. Among those to whom I am much indebted are Mr. Geoffrey Keynes, Blake's worthy bibliographer, both for his kindness in permitting me to make full use of his photographs of the pages of *Blake's MS. Book* and *The Pickering MS.*, and for almost every bibliographical fact given here; to Baron Dimsdale for personal facilities and permission to copy his example of *The Book of Urizen*; to Mr. W. A. White of New York for answers to many questions concerning his unique collection of Blake's books and pictures; to Mr. Joseph Wicksteed for valuable advice; to the authorities at the British Museum and the Fitzwilliam Museum, Cambridge, and to the home office.

The following bibliographical list may be helpful:

BIBLIOGRAPHY.—The Bibliography of William Blake, compiled by Geoffrey Keynes, was privately printed by the Grolier Club of New York in 1921. This valuable and exhaustive work contains detailed descriptions of all the differing copies of Blake's books now known to exist, as well as full reference to almost every publication concerning Blake.

WORKS PRINTED BY BLAKE HIMSELF.—There is No Natural Religion, 1788; All Religions are One, 1788; Songs of Innocence, 1789; The Book of Thel, 1789; The Marriage of Heaven and Hell, about 1793; Visions of the Daughters of Albion, 1793; America: a Prophecy, 1793; The Gates of Paradise (for Children), 1793; Prospectus to the Public, October 10, 1793; Songs of Experience, 1794; Europe: a Prophecy, 1794; The Book of Urizen, 1794; The Song of Los, 1795; The Book of Ahania, 1795; The Book of Los, 1795; Milton, about 1804–1809; Jerusalem, about 1804–1820; On Homer's Poetry: On Virgil, about 1818; the Laocoön Plate, about 1820; The Gates of Paradise (for the Sexes), about 1820; The Ghost of Abel, 1822.

WORKS PRINTED BY OTHERS DURING BLAKE'S LIFETIME.—Poetical Sketches, 1783; The French Revolution (not published), 1791; Advertisement of Exhibition of Paintings in Fresco, etc., 1809; A Descriptive Catalogue of Pictures, 1809; Prospectus of Engraving of Chaucer's Canterbury Pilgrims, 1809.

WORKS EXISTING ONLY IN MANUSCRIPT (excluding Annotations, Letters and Occasional Memoranda).—A Seven Page MS. of Metrical Prose, before 1777; An Island in the Moon (incomplete and unfinished), about 1787; Tiriel, about 1789; The Four Zoas, or Vala (complete, but not finally revised), 1797—about 1803; Blake's Manuscript Book (commonly known as " The Rossetti MS."), 1793—about 1820; A Twenty-two Page MS. of Poems (commonly known as " The Pickering MS."), about 1800.

WORKS UNKNOWN BUT PRESUMED TO HAVE EXISTED.—Barry: a Poem; The Book of Moonlight; Outhoun; The History of England, a small book of Engravings.

PRINCIPAL POSTHUMOUS EDITIONS.—Songs of Innocence and of Experience, with Memoir by J. J. Garth Wilkinson, 1839; Selections, edited by D. G. Rossetti, in vol. ii. of Gilchrist's Life of Blake (see below), 1863; Poetical Sketches, ed. by R. H. Shepherd, 1868; The Poetical Works of William Blake, with Memoir by W. M. Rossetti, 1874; Facsimile Reproductions of most of Blake's Poetical Works, hand-coloured, by W. Muir, 1884–1890; Facsimile Reproduction of Songs of Innocence and of Experience (54 plates), with Introduction by E. J. Ellis, 1893; The Works of William Blake, Poetic, Symbolic and Critical (mostly in lithographic facsimile), 3 vols., ed. with Memoir and Interpretation by E. J. Ellis and W. B. Yeats, 1893; The Poetical Works of William Blake, ed. by E. J. Ellis, 2 vols., 1906; Jerusalem, ed., with Introduction, by E. R. D. Maclagan and A. G. B. Russell, 1904, and Milton, ed. by same, 1907; The Engravings of William Blake, by A. G. B. Russell, 1912; The Poetical Works of William Blake, ed. with Bibliographical Notes and Prefaces by John Sampson (Clarendon), 1905; (Oxford), 1913; Lyrical Poems of William Blake, with Introduction by Walter Raleigh, 1905; The Writings of William Blake (a complete edition, including Letters, Annotations and all Memoranda), ed. by Geoffrey Keynes, 3 vols., 1925; The Prophetic Writings of William Blake, with Introduction, Glossary, etc., ed. by D. J. Sloss and J. P. R. Wallis, 2 vols. (Clarendon), 1926; Facsimile Reproduction of Poetical Sketches (British Museum copy), 1926; Facsimile Reproduction of Songs of Innocence ("Macgeorge" copy, British Museum), 1926.

LETTERS.—The Letters of William Blake (together with his Life, by F. Tatham), ed. by A. G. B. Russell, 1906; also, with additional Letters, in "Writings," ed. by Geoffrey Keynes, 1925 (see above); Facsimile Reproductions of Blake's Letters to Captain Butts, 1800–1803, ed. by Geoffrey Keynes, 1926.

BIOGRAPHIES.—A Father's Memoirs of his Child, by T. H. Malkin, 1806; Nollekens and his Times, by J. T. Smith, 1828; Lives of the most Eminent British Painters, by Allan Cunningham, 1830; The Life of William Blake, by F. Tatham (bound with the only finished copy of "Jerusalem," and first published with Blake's Letters, see above); Diary, Reminiscences and Correspondence of Henry Crabb Robinson, 1869; Life of William Blake, by Alexander Gilchrist, 1863, second enlarged edition, 1880.

CRITICAL STUDIES.—William Blake: A Critical Essay, by A. C. Swinburne, 1868; William Blake, Painter and Poet, by Richard Garnett, 1895; William Blake and his Illustrations to the Divine Comedy, by W. B. Yeats, first in "The Savoy," 1896, afterwards in "Ideas of Good and Evil," 1903; The Real Blake, by E. J. Ellis, 1907; William Blake, by Arthur Symons, 1907; Blake and his Æsthetic, in "Art and Life," by T. Sturge Moore, 1910; Blake's Vision of the Book of Job, by J. H. Wicksteed, 1910, enlarged edition, 1924; William Blake, by G. K. Chesterton, 1910; William Blake, Poet and Mystic, by P. Berger, English translation, 1914; William Blake, his Philosophy and Symbols, by S. Foster Damon, 1924; William Blake, by Ernest H. Short, 1925; The Paintings of William Blake, by Darrell Figgis, 1925; The Engraved Designs of William Blake, by Lawrence Binyon, 1926.

MAX PLOWMAN.

January 1927.

CONTENTS

II

FRAGMENTS FROM BLAKE'S MSS.

CONTENTS

III
POETICAL SKETCHES

I

WORKS
PRINTED AND ILLUSTRATED
BY BLAKE

THERE

is

NO NATURAL RELIGION

(1788)

[a]

The Argument

Man has no notion of moral fitness but from Education. Naturally he is only a natural organ subject to Sense.

I

Man cannot naturally Percieve but through his natural or bodily organs.

II

Man by his reasoning power can only compare & judge of what he has already perciev'd.

III

From a perception of only 3 senses or 3 elements none could deduce a fourth or fifth.

IV

None could have other than natural or organic thoughts if he had none but organic perceptions.

V

Man's desires are limited by his perceptions: none can desire what he has not perciev'd.

VI

The desires & perceptions of man untaught by any thing but organs of sense, must be limited to objects of sense.

Conclusion

If it were not for the Poetic or Prophetic Character, the Philosophic & Experimental would soon be at the ratio of all things & stand still, unable to do other than repeat the same dull round over again.

[b]

I

Man's perceptions are not bounded by organs of perception: he percieves more than sense (tho' ever so acute) can discover.

II

Reason, or the ratio of all we have already known, is not the same that it shall be when we know more.

III

[*This proposition is missing.*]

IV

The bounded is loathed by its possessor. The same dull round, even of a universe, would soon become a mill with complicated wheels.

V

If the many become the same as the few when possess'd, More! More! is the cry of a mistaken soul: less than All cannot satisfy Man.

VI

If any could desire what he is incapable of possessing, despair must be his eternal lot.

VII

The desire of Man being Infinite, the possession is Infinite & himself Infinite.

Application

He who sees the Infinite in all things, sees God. He who sees the Ratio only, sees himself only.

Therefore God becomes as we are, that we may be as he is.

ALL RELIGIONS are ONE
(1788)

The Voice of one crying in the Wilderness.

The Argument

As the true method of knowledge is experiment, the true faculty of knowing must be the faculty which experiences. This faculty I treat of.

Principle 1st

That the Poetic Genius is the true Man, and that the body or outward form of Man is derived from the Poetic Genius. Likewise that the forms of all things are derived from their Genius, which by the Ancients was call'd an Angel & Spirit & Demon.

Principle 2d

As all men are alike in outward form, So (and with the same infinite variety) all are alike in the Poetic Genius.

Principle 3d

No man can think, write, or speak from his heart, but he must intend truth. Thus all sects of Philosophy are from the Poetic Genius adapted to the weaknesses of every individual.

Principle 4

As none by traveling over known lands can find out the unknown, So, from already acquired knowledge, Man could not acquire more; therefore an universal Poetic Genius exists.

Principle 5

The Religions of all Nations are derived from each Nation's different reception of the Poetic Genius, which is every where call'd the Spirit of Prophecy.

Principle 6
The Jewish & Christian Testaments are An original derivation from the Poetic Genius: this is necessary from the confined nature of bodily sensation.

Principle 7
As all men are alike (tho' infinitely various), So all Religions, &, as all similars, have one source.
The true Man is the source, he being the Poetic Genius.

SONGS

Of

INNOCENCE

and Of

EXPERIENCE

Shewing the Two Contrary States
of the Human Soul

(1794)

SONGS of INNOCENCE

(1789)

Introduction

PIPING down the valleys wild,
Piping songs of pleasant glee,
On a cloud I saw a child,
And he laughing said to me:

" Pipe a song about a Lamb! "
So I piped with merry chear.
 " Piper, pipe that song again; "
So I piped: he wept to hear.

" Drop thy pipe, thy happy pipe,
Sing thy songs of happy chear."
So I sung the same again
While he wept with joy to hear.

" Piper, sit thee down and write
In a book that all may read."
So he vanish'd from my sight,
And I pluck'd a hollow reed,

And I made a rural pen,
And I stain'd the water clear,
And I wrote my happy songs
Every child may joy to hear.

The Shepherd

How sweet is the Shepherd's sweet lot!
From the morn to the evening he strays;
He shall follow his sheep all the day,
And his tongue shall be filled with praise.

For he hears the lambs' innocent call,
And he hears the ewes' tender reply;
He is watchful, while they are in peace
For they know when their Shepherd is nigh.

The Ecchoing Green

THE Sun does arise
And make happy the skies,
The merry bells ring
To welcome the Spring,
The sky-lark and thrush,
The birds of the bush,
Sing louder around
To the bells' chearful sound,
While our sports shall be seen
On the Ecchoing Green.

Old John with white hair
Does laugh away care,
Sitting under the oak
Among the old folk.
They laugh at our play,
And soon they all say:
" Such, such were the joys
When we all, girls & boys,

In our youth-time were seen
On the Ecchoing Green.''

Till the little ones, weary,
No more can be merry;
The sun does descend,
And our sports have an end.
Round the laps of their mothers
Many sisters and brothers,
Like birds in their nest,
Are ready for rest,
And sport no more seen
On the darkening Green.

The Lamb

LITTLE Lamb, who made thee?
　Dost thou know who made thee?
Gave thee life & bid thee feed
By the stream & o'er the mead;
Gave thee clothing of delight,
Softest clothing, wooly, bright;
Gave thee such a tender voice
Making all the vales rejoice?
　Little Lamb, who made thee?
　Dost thou know who made thee?

　Little Lamb, I'll tell thee,
　Little Lamb, I'll tell thee:
He is called by thy name,
For he calls himself a Lamb.
He is meek & he is mild;
He became a little child:
I a child & thou a lamb,
We are called by his name.
　Little Lamb, God bless thee.
　Little Lamb, God bless thee.

The Little Black Boy

My mother bore me in the southern wild,
And I am black, but O! my soul is white;
White as an angel is the English child,
But I am black, as if bereav'd of light.

My mother taught me underneath a tree,
And sitting down before the heat of day
She took me on her lap and kissed me,
And pointing to the east, began to say:

" Look on the rising sun! there God does live,
And gives his light and gives his heat away;
And flowers and trees and beasts and men recieve
Comfort in morning, joy in the noon day.

" And we are put on earth a little space
That we may learn to bear the beams of love;
And these black bodies and this sun-burnt face
Is but a cloud, and like a shady grove;

" For when our souls have learn'd the heat to bear,
The cloud will vanish: we shall hear his voice,
Saying: ' come out from the grove, my love & care,
And round my golden tent like lambs rejoice.' "

Thus did my mother say, and kissed me.
And thus I say to little English boy:
When I from black and he from white cloud free
And round the tent of God like lambs we joy,

I'll shade him from the heat, till he can bear
To lean in joy upon our father's knee;
And then I'll stand and stroke his silver hair,
And be like him, and he will then love me.

The Blossom

MERRY Merry Sparrow,
Under leaves so green,
A happy Blossom
Sees you swift as arrow
Seek your cradle narrow
Near my Bosom.

Pretty Pretty Robin,
Under leaves so green,
A happy Blossom
Hears you sobbing, sobbing,
Pretty Pretty Robin
Near my Bosom.

The Chimney Sweeper

WHEN my mother died I was very young,
And my father sold me while yet my tongue
Could scarcely cry ' weep, weep, weep, weep,'
So your chimneys I sweep & in soot I sleep.

There's little Tom Dacre who cried when his head,
That curl'd like a lamb's back, was shav'd: so I said,
" Hush, Tom, never mind it, for when your head's bare
You know that the soot cannot spoil your white hair."

And so he was quiet, & that very night,
As Tom was a sleeping, he had such a sight,
That thousands of sweepers, Dick, Joe, Ned & Jack,
Were all of them lock'd up in coffins of black.

And by came an Angel who had a bright key,
And he open'd the coffins & set them all free;
Then down a green plain, leaping, laughing, they run,
And wash in a river, and shine in the Sun.

Then naked & white, all their bags left behind,
They rise upon clouds, and sport in the wind;
And the Angel told Tom, if he'd be a good boy,
He'd have God for his father & never want joy.

And so Tom awoke; and we rose in the dark,
And got with our bags & our brushes to work.
Tho' the morning was cold, Tom was happy & warm;
So if all do their duty they need not fear harm.

The Little Boy lost

"FATHER, father, where are you going?
O do not walk so fast.
Speak father, speak to your little boy,
Or else I shall be lost."

The night was dark, no father was there;
The child was wet with dew;
The mire was deep, & the child did weep,
And away the vapour flew.

The Little Boy found

THE little boy lost in the lonely fen,
Led by the wand'ring light,
Began to cry, but God ever nigh,
Appear'd like his father in white.

He kissed the child & by the hand led
And to his mother brought,
Who in sorrow pale, thro' the lonely dale,
Her little boy weeping sought.

Laughing Song

WHEN the green woods laugh with the voice of joy,
And the dimpling stream runs laughing by,
When the air does laugh with our merry wit,
And the green hill laughs with the noise of it,

When the meadows laugh with lively green,
And the grasshopper laughs in the merry scene,
When Mary and Susan and Emily
With their sweet round mouths sing " Ha, Ha, He! "

When the painted birds laugh in the shade
Where our table with cherries and nuts is spread,
Come live & be merry and join with me,
To sing the sweet chorus of " Ha, Ha, He! "

A CRADLE SONG

SWEET dreams, form a shade
O'er my lovely infant's head,
Sweet dreams of pleasant streams
By happy silent moony beams.

Sweet sleep, with soft down
Weave thy brows an infant crown.
Sweet sleep, Angel mild,
Hover o'er my happy child.

Sweet smiles, in the night
Hover over my delight;
Sweet smiles, Mother's smiles,
All the livelong night beguiles.

Sweet moans, dovelike sighs
Chase not slumber from thy eyes.
Sweet moans, sweeter smiles
All the dovelike moans beguiles.

Sleep, sleep, happy child,
All creation slept and smil'd;
Sleep, sleep, happy sleep,
While o'er thee thy mother weep.

Sweet babe, in thy face
Holy image I can trace.
Sweet babe, once like thee
Thy maker lay and wept for me:

Wept for me, for thee, for all,
When he was an infant small.
Thou his image ever see,
Heavenly face that smiles on thee:

Smiles on thee, on me, on all,
Who became an infant small.
Infant smiles are his own smiles,
Heaven & earth to peace beguiles.

The Divine Image

To Mercy Pity Peace and Love
All pray in their distress,
And to these virtues of delight
Return their thankfulness.

For Mercy Pity Peace and Love
Is God our father dear,
And Mercy Pity Peace and Love
Is Man his child and care.

For Mercy has a human heart,
Pity, a human face,
And Love, the human form divine,
And Peace, the human dress.

Then every man of every clime
That prays in his distress,
Prays to the human form divine,
Love Mercy Pity Peace.

And all must love the human form
In heathen, turk or jew.
Where Mercy Love & Pity dwell
There God is dwelling too.

HOLY THURSDAY

'TWAS on a Holy Thursday, their innocent faces clean,
The children walking two & two, in red & blue & green,
Grey headed beadles walk'd before, with wands as white
as snow,
Till into the high dome of Paul's they like Thames' waters
flow.

O what a multitude they seem'd, these flowers of London
town!
Seated in companies they sit with radiance all their own.
The hum of multitudes was there, but multitudes of lambs,
Thousands of little boys & girls raising their innocent hands.

Now like a mighty wind they raise to heaven the voice of
song,
Or like harmonious thunderings the seats of heaven among.
Beneath them sit the aged men, wise guardians of the poor;
Then cherish pity, lest you drive an angel from your door.

Night

THE sun descending in the west
The evening star does shine,
The birds are silent in their nest
And I must seek for mine,
The moon, like a flower
In heaven's high bower,
With silent delight
Sits and smiles on the night.

Farewell green fields and happy groves
Where flocks have took delight;
Where lambs have nibbled, silent moves
The feet of angels bright;
Unseen they pour blessing
And joy without ceasing
On each bud and blossom
And each sleeping bosom.

They look in every thoughtless nest
Where birds are cover'd warm,
They visit caves of every beast
To keep them all from harm;
If they see any weeping
That should have been sleeping,
They pour sleep on their head
And sit down by their bed.

When wolves and tygers howl for prey
They pitying stand and weep,
Seeking to drive their thirst away
And keep them from the sheep;
But if they rush dreadful,
The angels most heedful
Recieve each mild spirit
New worlds to inherit.

And there the lion's ruddy eyes
Shall flow with tears of gold,
And pitying the tender cries
And walking round the fold
Saying, "wrath, by his meekness,
And by his health, sickness
Is driven away
From our immortal day.

"And now beside thee, bleating lamb,
I can lie down and sleep,
Or think on him who bore thy name,
Graze after thee and weep;
For, wash'd in life's river,
My bright mane for ever
Shall shine like the gold
As I guard o'er the fold."

Spring

SOUND the Flute!
Now it's mute.
Birds delight
Day and Night;
Nightingale
In the dale,
Lark in Sky,
Merrily,
Merrily, Merrily, to welcome in the Year.

Little Boy
Full of joy,
Little Girl
Sweet and small,
Cock does crow,
So do you;
Merry voice,
Infant noise,
Merrily, Merrily, to welcome in the Year.

Little Lamb
Here I am,
Come and lick
My white neck,
Let me pull
Your soft Wool,
Let me kiss
Your soft face;
Merrily, Merrily we welcome in the Year.

Nurse's Song

WHEN the voices of children are heard on the green
And laughing is heard on the hill,
My heart is at rest within my breast
And every thing else is still.

" Then come home, my children, the sun is gone down
And the dews of night arise;
Come, come, leave off play, and let us away
Till the morning appears in the skies."

" No, no, let us play, for it is yet day
And we cannot go to sleep;
Besides, in the sky the little birds fly
And the hills are all cover'd with sheep."

" Well, well, go & play till the light fades away
And then go home to bed."
The little ones leaped & shouted & laugh'd
And all the hills ecchoed.

Infant Joy

" I have no name:
I am but two days old."
What shall I call thee?
" I happy am,
Joy is my name."
Sweet joy befall thee!

Pretty joy!
Sweet joy but two days old,
Sweet joy I call thee:
Thou dost smile,
I sing the while
Sweet joy befall thee.

A Dream

ONCE a dream did weave a shade
O'er my Angel-guarded bed,
That an Emmet lost its way
Where on grass methought I lay.

Troubled, 'wilder'd and folorn,
Dark, benighted, travel-worn,
Over many a tangled spray,
All heart-broke I heard her say:

"O my children! do they cry?
Do they hear their father sigh?
Now they look abroad to see,
Now return and weep for me."

Pitying, I dropp'd a tear;
But I saw a glow-worm near,
Who replied: "What wailing wight
Calls the watchman of the night?

"I am set to light the ground,
While the beetle goes his round:
Follow now the beetle's hum;
Little wanderer, hie thee home."

On Another's Sorrow

CAN I see another's woe
And not be in sorrow too?
Can I see another's grief
And not seek for kind relief?

Can I see a falling tear
And not feel my sorrow's share?
Can a father see his child
Weep, nor be with sorrow fill'd?

Can a mother sit and hear
An infant groan an infant fear?
No, no never can it be,
Never, never can it be.

And can he who smiles on all
Hear the wren with sorrows small,
Hear the small bird's grief & care,
Hear the woes that infants bear,

And not sit beside the nest
Pouring pity in their breast,
And not sit the cradle near
Weeping tear on infant's tear,

And not sit both night & day
Wiping all our tears away?
O! no never can it be,
Never, never can it be.

He doth give his joy to all,
He becomes an infant small,
He becomes a man of woe,
He doth feel the sorrow too.

Think not thou canst sigh a sigh
And thy maker is not by;
Think not thou canst weep a tear
And thy maker is not near.

O! he gives to us his joy
That our grief he may destroy;
Till our grief is fled & gone
He doth sit by us and moan.

SONGS of EXPERIENCE
(1794)

Introduction

HEAR the voice of the Bard!
Who Present, Past, & Future sees,
Whose ears have heard
The Holy Word
That walk'd among the ancient trees,

Calling the lapsed Soul,
And weeping in the evening dew,
That might controll
The starry pole
And fallen fallen light renew!

" O Earth, O Earth return!
Arise from out the dewy grass;
Night is worn
And the morn
Rises from the slumberous mass.

" Turn away no more:
Why wilt thou turn away?
The starry floor
The wat'ry shore
Is giv'n thee till the break of day."

EARTH'S Answer

EARTH rais'd up her head
From the darkness dread & drear.
Her light fled:
Stony dread!
And her locks cover'd with grey despair.

" Prison'd on wat'ry shore,
Starry Jealousy does keep my den
Cold and hoar;
Weeping o'er,
I hear the father of the ancient men.

" Selfish father of men,
Cruel, jealous, selfish fear:
Can delight,
Chain'd in night,
The virgins of youth and morning bear?

" Does spring hide its joy
When buds and blossoms grow?
Does the sower
Sow by night?
Or the plowman in darkness plow?

" Break this heavy chain
That does freeze my bones around.
Selfish! vain!
Eternal bane!
That free Love with bondage bound."

The CLOD & the PEBBLE

" LOVE seeketh not Itself to please
Nor for itself hath any care,
But for another gives its ease
And builds a Heaven in Hell's despair."

    So sung a little Clod of Clay
    Trodden with the cattle's feet,
    But a Pebble of the brook
    Warbled out these metres meet:

" Love seeketh only Self to please,
To bind another to Its delight,
Joys in another's loss of ease,
And builds a Hell in Heaven's despite."

HOLY THURSDAY

Is this a holy thing to see
In a rich and fruitful land,
Babes reduc'd to misery,
Fed with cold and usurous hand?

Is that trembling cry a song?
Can it be a song of joy?
And so many children poor?
It is a land of poverty!

And their sun does never shine,
And their fields are bleak & bare,
And their ways are fill'd with thorns:
It is eternal winter there.

For where-e'er the sun does shine,
And where-e'er the rain does fall,
Babe can never hunger there,
Nor poverty the mind appall.

The Little Girl Lost

In futurity
I prophetic see
That the earth from sleep
(Grave the sentence deep)

Shall arise and seek
For her maker meek,
And the desart wild
Become a garden mild.

In the southern clime
Where the summer's prime
Never fades away,
Lovely Lyca lay.

Seven summers old
Lovely Lyca told;
She had wander'd long
Hearing wild birds' song.

" Sweet sleep, come to me
Underneath this tree.
Do father, mother, weep,
Where can Lyca sleep?

" Lost in desart wild
Is your little child.
How can Lyca sleep
If her mother weep?

" If her heart does ake
Then let Lyca wake;
If my mother sleep,
Lyca shall not weep.

" Frowning frowning night,
O'er this desart bright
Let thy moon arise
While I close my eyes."

Sleeping Lyca lay
While the beasts of prey,
Come from caverns deep,
View'd the maid asleep.

The kingly lion stood
And the virgin view'd,
Then he gambol'd round
O'er the hallow'd ground.

Leopards, tygers play
Round her as she lay,
While the lion old
Bow'd his mane of gold,

And her bosom lick,
And upon her neck
From his eyes of flame
Ruby tears there came;

While the lioness
Loos'd her slender dress,
And naked they convey'd
To caves the sleeping maid.

The Little Girl Found

ALL the night in woe
Lyca's parents go
Over vallies deep,
While the desarts weep.

Tired and woe-begone,
Hoarse with making moan,
Arm in arm seven days
They trac'd the desart ways.

Seven nights they sleep
Among shadows deep,
And dream they see their child
Starv'd in desart wild.

Pale, thro' pathless ways
The fancied image strays,
Famish'd, weeping, weak
With hollow piteous shriek.

Rising from unrest,
The trembling woman prest
With feet of weary woe:
She could no further go.

In his arms he bore
Her arm'd with sorrow sore,
Till before their way
A couching lion lay.

Turning back was vain:
Soon his heavy mane
Bore them to the ground,
Then he stalk'd around

Smelling to his prey,
But their fears allay
When he licks their hands
And silent by them stands

They look upon his eyes
Fill'd with deep surprise,
And wondering behold
A spirit arm'd in gold.

On his head a crown,
On his shoulders down
Flow'd his golden hair.
Gone was all their care.

" Follow me," he said;
" Weep not for the maid;
In my palace deep
Lyca lies asleep."

Then they followed
Where the vision led,
And saw their sleeping child
Among tygers wild.

To this day they dwell
In a lonely dell,
Nor fear the wolvish howl
Nor the lion's growl.

The Chimney Sweeper

A LITTLE black thing among the snow,
Crying ' weep, weep,' in notes of woe!
" Where are thy father & mother, say? "
" They are both gone up to the church to pray.

" Because I was happy upon the heath,
And smil'd among the winter's snow,
They clothed me in the clothes of death,
And taught me to sing the notes of woe.

" And because I am happy, & dance & sing,
They think they have done me no injury,
And are gone to praise God & his Priest & King,
Who make up a heaven of our misery."

NURSE'S Song

WHEN the voices of children are heard on the green
And whisp'rings are in the dale,
The days of my youth rise fresh in my mind:
My face turns green and pale.

Then come home my children, the sun is gone down
And the dews of night arise;
Your spring & your day are wasted in play,
And your winter and night in disguise.

The SICK ROSE

O ROSE, thou art sick:
The invisible worm
That flies in the night
In the howling storm,

Has found out thy bed
Of crimson joy,
And his dark secret love
Does thy life destroy.

THE FLY

LITTLE Fly,
Thy summer's play
My thoughtless hand
Has brush'd away.

Am not I
A fly like thee?
Or art not thou
A man like me?

For I dance
And drink & sing,
Till some blind hand
Shall brush my wing.

If thought is life
And strength & breath,
And the want
Of thought is death,

Then am I
A happy fly
If I live
Or if I die.

The Angel

I DREAMT a Dream! what can it mean?
And that I was a maiden Queen
Guarded by an Angel mild:
Witless woe was ne'er beguil'd!

And I wept both night and day,
And he wip'd my tears away,
And I wept both day and night,
And hid from him my heart's delight.

So he took his wings and fled;
Then the morn blush'd rosy red;
I dried my tears & arm'd my fears
With ten thousand shields and spears.

Soon my Angel came again:
I was arm'd, he came in vain,
For the time of youth was fled
And grey hairs were on my head.

The Tyger

TYGER, Tyger, burning bright
In the forests of the night,
What immortal hand or eye
Could frame thy fearful symmetry?

In what distant deeps or skies
Burnt the fire of thine eyes?
On what wings dare he aspire?
What the hand dare sieze the fire?

And what shoulder, & what art,
Could twist the sinews of thy heart?
And when thy heart began to beat,
What dread hand? & what dread feet?

What the hammer? what the chain,
In what furnace was thy brain?
What the anvil? what dread grasp
Dare its deadly terrors clasp?

When the stars threw down their spears
And water'd heaven with their tears,
Did he smile his work to see?
Did he who made the Lamb make thee?

Tyger, Tyger, burning bright
In the forests of the night,
What immortal hand or eye
Dare frame thy fearful symmetry?

My Pretty ROSE TREE

A FLOWER was offer'd to me,
Such a flower as May never bore;
But I said " I've a Pretty Rose-tree,"
And I passed the sweet flower o'er.

Then I went to my Pretty Rose-tree,
To tend her by day and by night;
But my Rose turn'd away with jealousy,
And her thorns were my only delight.

AH! SUN-FLOWER

Ah Sun-flower! weary of time,
Who countest the steps of the Sun,
Seeking after that sweet golden clime
Where the traveller's journey is done:

Where the Youth pined away with desire,
And the pale Virgin shrouded in snow,
Arise from their graves and aspire
Where my Sun-flower wishes to go.

THE LILLY

THE modest Rose puts forth a thorn,
The humble Sheep a threat'ning horn,
While the Lilly white shall in Love delight,
Nor a thorn nor a threat stain her beauty bright.

The GARDEN of LOVE

I WENT to the Garden of Love,
And saw what I never had seen:
A Chapel was built in the midst,
Where I used to play on the green.

And the gates of this Chapel were shut,
And ' Thou shalt not ' writ over the door;
So I turn'd to the Garden of Love
That so many sweet flowers bore;

And I saw it was filled with graves,
And tomb-stones where flowers should be;
And Priests in black gowns were walking their rounds,
And binding with briars my joys & desires.

The Little Vagabond

DEAR Mother, dear Mother, the Church is cold,
But the Ale-house is healthy & pleasant & warm;
Besides I can tell where I am used well,
Such usage in heaven will never do well.

But if at the Church they would give us some Ale
And a pleasant fire our souls to regale,
We'd sing and we'd pray all the live-long day,
Nor ever once wish from the Church to stray.

Then the Parson might preach & drink & sing,
And we'd be as happy as birds in the spring;
And modest dame Lurch, who is always at Church,
Would not have bandy children, nor fasting, nor birch.

And God, like a father rejoicing to see
His children as pleasant and happy as he,
Would have no more quarrel with the Devil or the Barrel,
But kiss him & give him both drink and apparel.

LONDON

I WANDER thro' each charter'd street
Near where the charter'd Thames does flow,
And mark in every face I meet
Marks of weakness, marks of woe.

In every cry of every Man,
In every Infant's cry of fear,
In every voice, in every ban,
The mind-forg'd manacles I hear.

How the Chimney-sweeper's cry
Every black'ning Church appalls,
And the hapless Soldier's sigh
Runs in blood down Palace walls.

But most thro' midnight streets I hear
How the youthful Harlot's curse
Blasts the new born Infant's tear,
And blights with plagues the Marriage hearse.

The Human Abstract

PITY would be no more
If we did not make somebody Poor;
And Mercy no more could be
If all were as happy as we.

And mutual fear brings peace,
Till the selfish loves increase:
Then Cruelty knits a snare
And spreads his baits with care.

He sits down with holy fears
And waters the ground with tears:
Then Humility takes its root
Underneath his foot.

Soon spreads the dismal shade
Of Mystery over his head,
And the Catterpiller and Fly
Feed on the Mystery.

And it bears the fruit of Deceit,
Ruddy and sweet to eat,
And the Raven his nest has made
In its thickest shade.

The Gods of the earth and sea
Sought thro' Nature to find this Tree,
But their search was all in vain:
There grows one in the Human Brain.

INFANT SORROW

My mother groan'd! my father wept,
Into the dangerous world I leapt,
Helpless, naked, piping loud,
Like a fiend hid in a cloud.

Struggling in my father's hands,
Striving against my swadling bands,
Bound and weary, I thought best
To sulk upon my mother's breast.

A POISON TREE

I was angry with my friend,
I told my wrath, my wrath did end;
I was angry with my foe,
I told it not, my wrath did grow.

And I water'd it in fears,
Night & morning with my tears;
And I sunned it with smiles,
And with soft deceitful wiles.

And it grew both day and night,
Till it bore an apple bright;
And my foe beheld it shine,
And he knew that it was mine,

And into my garden stole
When the night had veil'd the pole:
In the morning glad I see
My foe outstretch'd beneath the tree.

A Little BOY Lost[1]

" NOUGHT loves another as itself,
Nor venerates another so,
Nor is it possible to Thought
A greater than itself to know:

" And Father, how can I love you
Or any of my brothers more?
I love you like the little bird
That picks up crumbs around the door."

The Priest sat by and heard the child,
In trembling zeal he siez'd his hair:
He led him by his little coat,
And all admir'd the Priestly care.

And standing on the altar high,
" Lo, what a fiend is here! " said he,
" One who sets reason up for judge
Of our most holy Mystery."

The weeping child could not be heard,
The weeping parents wept in vain;
They strip'd him to his little shirt,
And bound him in an iron chain;

And burn'd him in a holy place,
Where many had been burn'd before:
The weeping parents wept in vain.
Are such things done on Albion's shore?

---

[1] See note on p. 381.

A Little GIRL Lost

Children of the future Age
Reading this indignant page,
Know that in a former time
Love! sweet Love! was thought a crime.

IN the Age of Gold,
Free from winter's cold,
Youth and maiden bright
To the holy light,
Naked in the sunny beams delight.

Once a youthful pair,
Fill'd with softest care,
Met in garden bright
Where the holy light
Had just remov'd the curtains of the night.

There, in rising day,
On the grass they play;
Parents were afar,
Strangers came not near,
And the maiden soon forgot her fear.

Tired with kisses sweet,
They agree to meet
When the silent sleep
Waves o'er heaven's deep,
And the weary tired wanderers weep.

To her father white
Came the maiden bright;
But his loving look,
Like the holy book,
All her tender limbs with terror shook.

"Ona! pale and weak!
To thy father speak:
O the trembling fear!
O the dismal care!
That shakes the blossoms of my hoary hair."

To Tirzah

WHATE'ER is Born of Mortal Birth
Must be consumed with the Earth
To rise from Generation free:
Then what have I to do with thee?

The Sexes sprung from Shame & Pride,
Blow'd in the morn, in evening died;
But Mercy chang'd Death into Sleep;
The Sexes rose to work & weep.

Thou Mother of my Mortal part,
With cruelty didst mould my Heart,
And with false self-decieving tears
Didst bind my Nostrils Eyes & Ears:

Didst close my Tongue in senseless clay,
And me to Mortal Life betray.
The Death of Jesus set me free:[1]
Then what have I to do with thee?

The School Boy

I LOVE to rise in a summer morn
When the birds sing on every tree;
The distant huntsman winds his horn,
And the sky-lark sings with me.
O! what sweet company.

But to go to school in a summer morn,
O! it drives all joy away;
Under a cruel eye outworn
The little ones spend the day
In sighing and dismay.

[1] It is Raised a Spiritual Body.

This quotation from I. Corinth. xv. 44, is inscribed by Blake on one of the figures of the illustration to this poem.

Ah! then at times I drooping sit,
And spend many an anxious hour,
Nor in my book can I take delight,
Nor sit in learning's bower,
Worn thro' with the dreary shower.

How can the bird that is born for joy
Sit in a cage and sing?
How can a child when fears annoy
But droop his tender wing
And forget his youthful spring?

O! father & mother, if buds are nip'd
And blossoms blown away,
And if the tender plants are strip'd
Of their joy in the springing day,
By sorrow and care's dismay,

How shall the summer arise in joy,
Or the summer fruits appear?
Or how shall we gather what griefs destroy,
Or bless the mellowing year
When the blasts of winter appear?

The Voice of the Ancient Bard

YOUTH of delight, come hither
And see the opening morn,
Image of truth new born.
Doubt is fled & clouds of reason,
Dark disputes & artful teazing.
Folly is an endless maze,
Tangled roots perplex her ways,
How many have fallen there!
They stumble all night over bones of the dead,
And feel they know not what but care,
And wish to lead others when they should be led.

NOTE.—*Blake etched the following poem upon a copper plate in his usual manner, but as he never included the verses in any copy of the Songs of Experience they may safely be regarded as having been rejected by him.*

A Divine Image

CRUELTY has a Human Heart,
And Jealousy a Human Face;
Terror the Human Form Divine,
And Secrecy the Human Dress.

The Human Dress is forged Iron,
The Human Form a fiery Forge,
The Human Face a Furnace seal'd,
The Human Heart its hungry Gorge.

THE
BOOK OF THEL

(1789)

THEL'S Motto

DOES the Eagle know what is in the pit?
Or wilt thou go ask the Mole:
Can Wisdom be put in a silver rod?
Or Love in a golden bowl?

I

THE daughters of [1] Mne Seraphim led round their sunny flocks,
All but the youngest: she in paleness sought the secret air,
To fade away like morning beauty from her mortal day;
Down by the river of Adona her soft voice is heard,
And thus her gentle lamentation falls like morning dew: 5

"O life of this our spring! why fades the lotus of the water?
Why fade these children of the spring? born but to smile & fall.
Ah! Thel is like a wat'ry bow, and like a parting cloud,
Like a reflection in a glass, like shadows in the water,
Like dreams of infants, like a smile upon an infant's face,   10
Like the dove's voice, like transient day, like music in the air.
Ah! gentle may I lay me down and gentle rest my head,
And gentle sleep the sleep of death, and gentle hear the voice
Of him that walketh in the garden in the evening time."

The Lilly of the Valley, breathing in the humble grass,   15
Answer'd the lovely maid and said: "I am a wat'ry weed,
And I am very small and love to dwell in lowly vales,
So weak the gilded butterfly scarce perches on my head;

---

[1] "In the list of spirits in Agrippa's *Occult Philosophy*, II. xxii., from which Blake took the names *Tiriel* and *Zazel*, occurs the name *Bne Seraphim* (the sons of the Seraphim), who represent 'the Intelligencies of Venus.' It is reasonable to suppose that Blake intended to use this name, but made a mistake in the engraving which he could not correct. The change of *Bne* to *Mne* is apparently meaningless."—S. FOSTER DAMON, *William Blake: His Philosophy and Symbols.*

Yet I am visited from heaven, and he that smiles on all   19
Walks in the valley, and each morn over me spreads his hand
Saying, ' rejoice, thou humble grass, thou new-born lilly flower,
Thou gentle maid of silent valleys and of modest brooks;
For thou shalt be clothed in light, and fed with morning manna,
Till summer's heat melts thee beside the fountains and the springs
To flourish in eternal vales ': then why should Thel complain?
Why should the mistress of the vales of Har utter a sigh? "   26

She ceas'd & smil'd in tears, then sat down in her silver shrine.

Thel answer'd: " O thou little virgin of the peaceful valley,
Giving to those that cannot crave, the voiceless, the o'ertired;
Thy breath doth nourish the innocent lamb, he smells thy milky
          garments,
He crops thy flowers while thou sittest smiling in his face,   31
Wiping his mild and meekin mouth from all contagious taints.
Thy wine doth purify the golden honey; thy perfume,
Which thou dost scatter on every little blade of grass that springs,
Revives the milked cow, & tames the fire-breathing steed.   35
But Thel is like a faint cloud kindled at the rising sun:
I vanish from my pearly throne, and who shall find my place? "

" Queen of the vales," the Lilly answer'd, " ask the tender cloud
And it shall tell thee why it glitters in the morning sky,
And why it scatters its bright beauty thro' the humid air.   40
Descend, O little cloud, & hover before the eyes of Thel."

The Cloud descended, and the Lilly bow'd her modest head
And went to mind her numerous charge among the verdant grass.

II

" O little Cloud," the virgin said, " I charge thee tell to me
Why thou complainest not when in one hour thou fade away:
Then we shall seek thee, but not find: ah! Thel is like to thee:
I pass away: yet I complain, and no one hears my voice."

The Cloud then shew'd his golden head & his bright form emerg'd,
Hovering and glittering on the air before the face of Thel.   6

" O virgin, know'st thou not, our steeds drink of the golden springs
Where Luvah doth renew his horses: look'st thou on my youth,
And fearest thou, because I vanish and am seen no more,
Nothing remains? O maid, I tell thee, when I pass away,   10
It is to tenfold life, to love, to peace, and raptures holy
Unseen descending weigh my light wings upon balmy flowers

And court the fair eyed dew to take me to her shining tent:
The weeping virgin, trembling kneels before the risen sun,
Till we arise, link'd in a golden band, and never part,   15
But walk united, bearing food to all our tender flowers."

" Dost thou, O little Cloud? I fear that I am not like thee,
For I walk thro' the vales of Har, and smell the sweetest flowers,
But I feed not the little flowers. I hear the warbling birds,
But I feed not the warbling birds: they fly and seek their food:
But Thel delights in these no more, because I fade away;   21
And all shall say, ' without a use this shining woman liv'd,
Or did she only live to be at death the food of worms? ' "

The Cloud reclin'd upon his airy throne and answer'd thus:

" Then if thou art the food of worms, O virgin of the skies,   25
How great thy use, how great thy blessing! every thing that lives
Lives not alone, nor for itself: fear not, and I will call
The weak worm from its lowly bed, and thou shalt hear its voice.
Come forth, worm of the silent valley, to thy pensive queen."

The helpless worm arose and sat upon the Lilly's leaf,   30
And the bright Cloud sail'd on, to find his partner in the vale.

III

Then Thel astonish'd view'd the Worm upon its dewy bed.

" Art thou a Worm? image of weakness, art thou but a Worm?
I see thee like an infant wrapped in the Lilly's leaf.
Ah, weep not, little voice, thou canst not speak, but thou canst
        weep.
Is this a Worm? I see thee lay helpless & naked, weeping   5
And none to answer, none to cherish thee with mother's smiles."

The Clod of Clay heard the Worm's voice & rais'd her pitying head.
She bow'd over the weeping infant, and her life exhal'd
In milky fondness: then on Thel she fix'd her humble eyes.

" O beauty of the vales of Har, we live not for ourselves.   10
Thou seest me the meanest thing, and so I am indeed:
My bosom of itself is cold and of itself is dark,
But he that loves the lowly, pours his oil upon my head
And kisses me, and binds his nuptial bands around my breast,
And says: ' Thou mother of my children, I have loved thee,   15
And I have given thee a crown that none can take away.'
But how this is, sweet maid, I know not, and I cannot know;
I ponder, and I cannot ponder; yet I live and love."

The daughter of beauty wip'd her pitying tears with her white
    veil,
And said: " Alas! I knew not this, and therefore did I weep.   20
That God would love a Worm I knew, and punish the evil foot
That wilful bruis'd its helpless form; but that he cherish'd it
With milk and oil I never knew, and therefore did I weep;
And I complain'd in the mild air, because I fade away   24
And lay me down in thy cold bed, and leave my shining lot."

" Queen of the vales," the matron Clay answer'd, " I heard thy
    sighs,
And all thy moans flew o'er my roof, but I have call'd them down.
Wilt thou, O Queen, enter my house? 'tis given thee to enter
And to return: fear nothing, enter with thy virgin feet."   29

IV

The eternal gates' terrific porter lifted the northern bar.
Thel enter'd in & saw the secrets of the land unknown.
She saw the couches of the dead, & where the fibrous roots
Of every heart on earth infixes deep its restless twists:
A land of sorrows & of tears where never smile was seen.   5

She wander'd in the land of clouds thro' valleys dark, list'ning
Dolours and lamentations; waiting oft beside a dewy grave
She stood in silence, list'ning to the voices of the ground,
Till to her own grave plot she came, & there she sat down,
And heard this voice of sorrow breathed from the hollow pit: 10

" Why cannot the Ear be closed to its own destruction?
Or the glist'ning Eye to the poison of a smile!
Why are Eyelids stor'd with arrows ready drawn,
Where a thousand fighting men in ambush lie,
Or an Eye of gifts & graces show'ring fruits & coined gold?   15
Why a Tongue impress'd with honey from every wind?
Why an Ear, a whirlpool fierce to draw creations in?
Why a Nostril wide inhaling terror trembling & affright?
Why a tender curb upon the youthful burning boy?
Why a little curtain of flesh on the bed of our desire? "   20

The Virgin started from her seat, & with a shriek
Fled back unhinder'd till she came into the vales of Har.

The End

THE MARRIAGE

OF

HEAVEN AND HELL

(About 1793)

The Argument

RINTRAH roars & shakes his fires in the burden'd air;
Hungry clouds swag on the deep.

Once meek, and in a perilous path,
The just man kept his course along
The vale of death.
Roses are planted where thorns grow,
And on the barren heath
Sing the honey bees.

Then the perilous path was planted,
And a river and a spring
On every cliff and tomb,
And on the bleached bones
Red clay brought forth;

Till the villain left the paths of ease,
To walk in perilous paths, and drive
The just man into barren climes.

Now the sneaking serpent walks
In mild humility,
And the just man rages in the wilds
Where lions roam.

Rintrah roars & shakes his fires in the burden'd air;
Hungry clouds swag on the deep.